ALSO IN THE BLASTA BOOKS SERIES

Blasta Books #1: Tacos

Blasta Books #2: Hot Fat

Blasta Books #3: The United Nations of Cookies

Blasta Books #4: Wok

Blasta Books #5: Soup

Blasta Books #6: Tapas

Blasta Books #7: Wasted

blastabooks.com

MASARAP

Richie Castillo & Alex O'Neill

CONTENTS

Introduction 1
The Bahay manifesto 4
Salty, sour, sweet 4
Filipino pantry staples 8

Chicken
Banana ketchup-glazed wings 14
Adobo 16
Inihaw na manok (grilled chicken) 18
Chicken inasal 20
Filipino-style 4 in 1 22

Beef
Kare-kare (oxtail stew with peanut sauce) 24
Tiyula itum (burnt coconut beef) 26
Satti na curry (grilled beef skewers) 28
Bistek (Filly cheesesteak) 30

Pork
Filipino-style ribs 33
Lechon kawali (fried pork belly) 34
Tocino (cured sweet pork) 36
Lechon (pork belly) 37
Crispy pata (crispy fried ham hock) 38

Seafood

Kinilaw (cured fish) 40
Pancit na hipon (noodles with shrimp sauce) 42
Sinigang tahong (sour soup with mussels) 44

Rice

Sinangag (garlic rice) 46
How to cook and chill leftover rice safely 47
Lugaw (savoury rice porridge) 48

Snacks & sides

Sinigang potato crisps 49
Lumpia (pork spring rolls) 50
Filipino feasts 53
Laing (kale braised in coconut milk & chilli) 54
Poqui poqui (roasted aubergines & eggs) 55
Atchara (pickled green papaya) 56
Bagoong XO 58
Palapa (toasted coconut spice paste) 59

Sweet ending

Leche flan 60
Filly libre 62
White Filipino 62
A love letter to Filipino food and the
people who cook it 64

Index 66

INTRODUCTION

I was born in Dublin. My mother is Irish but was born in Jordan, as my grandfather worked in the UN as a field service officer. My Irish grandparents are originally from Annascaul, Kerry. My father was born in Manila, Philippines, and his father (my grandfather), also worked for the UN as a radio operator. My parents both spent time growing up in the Middle East and my mother even lived in the Congo briefly. My parents met and got married in Jerusalem and moved to London, where my sister was born. Fast forward four years and they were living in Ireland when I came along.

As you can see, my family is quite the multicultural mix. I often refer to myself as halo-halo, which means 'mix-mix' in Tagalog, as that's exactly how I feel. I'm a mixture of the different experiences, cultures and backgrounds that have shaped me into the person I am today.

I grew up in Dublin and travelled back to the Philippines every two years. I don't have many memories of my travels from when I was very young, just old family photos to go off. I was too young to really appreciate the Philippines and I guess that subconsciously, I wasn't proud of my heritage either.

Growing up, I didn't have any mixed-race or foreign friends. I was the only one in my area. You could count the number of mixed-race or foreign students in my entire school on two hands. When you're young, you definitely don't want to feel like the odd one out, which was one of the reasons I didn't want to embrace my Filipino heritage. Most people don't assume that I'm Irish *or* Filipino. You wouldn't believe how many times I get asked where I'm from and I still get strange looks when I say that I'm from Dublin.

Since both of my parents grew up away from their native countries, there was never any real affiliation to either Ireland or the Philippines in my house. This fostered a disconnection from my own cultural identity – but the one cultural outlet that has always been present in my life is food. Every day after school, my grandparents would pick me up and I would go back to their house for lunch and to do my homework. Bacon and cabbage, beef stew, chicken Kiev and mash, even a chicken curry from time to time – this was my exposure to Irish food and cooking.

My father was a nurse, but he's a phenomenal cook. He's the reason why I started to cook in the first place. He would cook such a wide variety of food, including Filipino classics like adobo, pancit, sinigang and kare-kare. Funnily enough, when I was younger I wasn't too keen on sinigang and things like bagoong, a fermented shrimp paste. I'm the opposite now; I absolutely love the stuff! But eating Filipino food was the one constant connection I had to the Philippines. Food was always celebrated in my house and we always sat down to share the meal together.

After school I went on to do a degree in social science. While studying, I got a job washing dishes in a local golf club. I soon began preparing and cooking food in the kitchen. After completing my degree, I moved to New Zealand for a year and continued to work in kitchens. Upon returning to Ireland I took a job at a local café and soon fell into the head chef role. It was a sink-or-swim scenario, but it worked out for the better in the end. After a year, I felt that I needed to move to a restaurant as I needed to learn and couldn't teach myself anything more. I worked in that restaurant for almost a year, then covid hit.

Overnight, I was let go. Just like that, my career turned to dust. The pandemic highlighted how disposable I was in the industry working for someone else. I felt there was a real lack of humility when covid hit in regard to how restaurants treated their staff. It made me realise that it wasn't the kind of industry I wanted to go back to work in unless I was working for myself.

Alex and I moved back to my parents' house during covid. We ate so much Filipino food during that time, since my father was always cooking for us. This is how the idea of Bahay started to formulate. When I knew I wanted to do something for myself, Filipino food was obviously the first thing that came to mind, seeing as how there was nowhere in Dublin serving Filipino food. The initial idea was to operate at markets with a food truck, but that plan soon fell to the wayside after we did our first pop-up at Roe & Co. The pop-up was a huge success and for many people, it was their first time trying Filipino food. Since then, we've gone from strength to strength, continuing to do pop-ups, markets and festivals.

For me, Bahay has been an outlet to express myself creatively. But it has also become much more than that. It has opened up a whole new world to me, a cultural aspect of my heritage that I had been so disconnected from.

MASARAP

The recipes in this book are by no means traditional or 'authentic'. For me, authenticity is completely subjective to the individual in the sense that what is authentic differs from person to person. This book is a collection of recipes that reflect my current journey into Filipino food. I'm really only scraping the surface of the rich culinary history that the Philippines has to offer. I could write hundreds of pages on the nuanced regional foods of the Philippines. Maybe another time.

Bahay has outgrown all my expectations. It started out as a covid lockdown project, but it has become the catalyst for me to connect with my Irish and Filipino identity through the cultural lens of food. It's helping me carve out my own bicultural identity and allowing me to present Filipino food to a wider audience. I've also met three other Irish-Filipinos through Bahay and, strangely enough, we're all weirdly similar in some unexpected ways. It was the first time in my life that I saw myself reflected back to me. It was the first time I felt seen. I'd never had that experience before and never knew I needed it.

I'm grateful to Alex and my family for being so supportive and allowing me to pursue my dreams and to all my friends and the people who have eaten our food or given us a dig-out at some of our events. I am eternally grateful as Bahay wouldn't be what it is today if it weren't for you.

Salamat!

SALTY, SOUR, SWEET

Filipino cuisine is dominated by the bold, brazen balance of three predominant and demanding elements of taste: salty, sour and sweet. These three monsters of flavour reign when it comes to Filipino cooking and make Filipino flavours addictive, exciting and compelling. More often than not, I feel my mouth pucker and water as my taste-buds catch up with the flavour explosion as the sour calamansi, sweet, spicy vinegar and salty tang of bagoong hit. Trying some of these foods reminds me of when I first tried wasabi. It's like a punch in the face that shocks you, then immediately makes you want to experience it again and again. No? Just me?

Filipinos love snacking on tart green mangos and red onion topped with salty, funky (often sweet or caramelised) bagoong, which gives a hit of salty, sour and sweet flavours and is often eaten as a palate cleanser. It's a little like melon and Parma ham, in a weirdly familiar way.

Overall, the combination of sugar, salt and acid in Filipino cuisine creates a balance of flavours that is unmistakably Filipino and unapologetically delicious. These flavours have been shaped by a medley of cultural, historical and environmental influences that have shaped Filipino culinary traditions for centuries.

SALTY

Filipinos love salt. Salt is a key flavour in Filipino cuisine, both to highlight other flavours but also as a standalone taste. Filipino soy sauce is extra salty, while Filipino snacks like chicharron, dilis (fried dried anchovies) and puffed fish crackers are loaded with salt. You'll often see salty cheese added to desserts and cakes to add a savoury element to sweets. While you may not always see salt on the dinner table, bowls of sawsawan (a Filipino soy dressing) and dishes of bagoong are both used as a table seasoning to add extra saltiness to shared pots of stews, fish and other dishes so that each person can season it to their taste.

Salt is also an important part of native Filipino cultural heritage for the Bohol people specifically. In this region, they make a native salt called asín tibuok. It's one of the rarest salts in the world. It's a sharp, earthy-tasting salt with smoky undertones, the flavour of which blew our minds when we tried it on our travels.

Making asín tibuok is a long, complex process that was created in the 7th century and has been passed down from generation to generation. The native salt-making method involves soaking coconut husks in seawater for months, then burning them slowly for several days with native hardwoods. The resulting coconut charcoal is then used as a filter for saltwater, making a concentrated brine that is poured continuously for hours at a time into simmering clay pots that are heated over an open fire to let the water evaporate, leaving the salt behind to crystallise in the rounded pots. The saltwater is added continuously until the pot is filled with hardened salt and the bottom of the pot cracks. The final product is a solid dome of salt.

The art of making asín tibuok has been declining and it was globally recognised as an endangered heritage food in 2016. Thankfully more supports are now there to help protect it, and thus more producers are looking into continuing this traditional salt-making practice.

SOUR

Mouth-watering, jolting acidity is not only acceptable in Filipino cooking, it's revered.

Acidic ingredients such as vinegars, calamansi and tamarind are vital components of Filipino cooking that are used to enhance the flavours of dishes and ingredients, to brighten up heavy dishes, to tenderise meats and used as a palate cleanser with unripe fruits and pickles (like the atchara on page 56).

While sourness is loved as a flavour, the high acidity also has a purpose beyond taste. The hot, wet, tropical climate of the Philippines can cause foods to spoil quickly, so using vinegar and other acidic ingredients is key for food preservation. The high acidity in adobo and sinigang means that pots can be left out on tables all day without worrying about spoiling. We've seen this first-hand on our travels.

SWEET

Filipinos have a major sweet tooth. Sweet treats were always popular, but the arrival of the Americans in 1898 escalated this even further. You'll find American doughnut shops and sugar-obsessed fast food chains scattered all over the place. But it's not just a US influence. You'll also see Filipino cake shops on every corner with lines out the door for special occasions and holidays. No dinner table is complete without an elaborate cake and dessert section to be devoured after the savoury feast.

The Philippines is a major world producer of sugar cane, which explains its popularity somewhat. The history of sugar cane production in the Philippines pre-dates Spanish colonisation, but this is when the industry really ramped up production. It can also be assumed that sugar is used as a preservative, just like acid.

Sugar is everywhere in Filipino cooking, not just in desserts. Traditional sweets like leche flan, halo-halo, biko, banana cue and bibingka are filled with sugar, but it's also used in savoury dishes like adobo, tocino, longanisa and (most controversially for global audiences) in spaghetti sauce.

You will be hard pressed to find coffee that isn't pre-sweetened, and teas and juices are usually filled with syrups and sugar. Sugar cane vinegar is probably the most popular Pinoy vinegar and you'll find it in most Asian stores. Basically, sugar is everywhere!

THE BAHAY MANIFESTO

We at Bahay believe food is universal. It transcends all languages and barriers. It features in all cultures and identities, but it's a particularly important part of the rich history of the Philippines.

Food is emotional. Food is nostalgic. Food is identity. Food is culture. Food is a way to connect with your cultural identity and can often be a way to identify yourself, your family and where you come from.

As Linda Civitello noted in *Cuisine and Culture: A History of Food and People*, food culture is a strong indicator of an identity: 'identity – religious, national, ethnic – is intensely bound up with food'.

Food communicates messages – the deep structures of the cultural life of people. Food communicates backgrounds, identities, lifestyles, likes and dislikes as well as other social and societal positions. Food, therefore, is a language that expresses the content of culture and the identity of a people. What does this remind us of? Art.

We think food – and expression through food – is an art in and of itself. We believe creativity manifests in many different ways, and the recent focus on food and cooking as a creative outlet has been transformative in the past decade.

FILIPINO PANTRY STAPLES

ALIGUE
Aligue is basically crab fat and is a Filipino speciality. Delicious, fatty and terrible for your cholesterol, use it sparingly! It's very hard to get here in Ireland, but we often pick up a jar of crab paste as a close alternative.

ANNATTO
This smoky spice that comes in seed form is used for flavouring and colour. It tastes earthy and peppery and is a bit like nutmeg. It was brought over by the Spanish, who, not content with colonising most of South America, went across the Pacific and colonised the Philippines for 333 years. It's used in stews like kare-kare, chicken inasal and palabok, mainly for its vibrant colour.

BAGOONG
This pungent crimson paste is bold, brash and fairly jazzy. Bagoong, which translates as 'fermented', is a fermented fish paste that comes in many varieties that are found across the Philippines. Bagoong's complex taste and combination of salty, sweet and umami flavours make it a staple in the Filipino kitchen.

Our favourite one is the caramelised version, which you can pick up in many Asian markets across Ireland. It's used as a table seasoning with bowls of kare-kare (peanut stew) and pinakbet (vegetable stew), which are seasoned to the diner's own taste, or eaten with unripe green mango, which is kind of like a Pinoy version of Parma ham and melon. We like to make bagoong rice by frying day-old leftover rice with bagoong and spring onions. It can be sweet, spicy or straight-up salty. Get yourself a jar, you won't regret it.

BANANA KETCHUP
We couldn't write a guide to Filipino flavours without including the OG, banana ketchup. We love this so much that we put it on the cover and we're excited to be producing our own line.

The name entices many, confuses some and disgusts a few. Banana ketchup is made from bananas, vinegar, sugar and spices. It's bright red, fruity, sweet and tangy. But why banana? Banana ketchup came about after the Americans introduced tomato ketchup, which the sweet-loving, condiment-obsessed Filipinos instantly fell in love with. However, when World War Two closed the Pacific Ocean for trade, there was a shortage of regular ketchup and tomatoes. This forced Filipinos to make their own alternative with what they had plenty of: bananas.

Banana ketchup was created by María Orosa, a Filipina food scientist, humanitarian and nationalist who was a pioneer in methods of preservation and the utilisation of native, indigenous ingredients and produce that had long been dismissed and scorned after centuries of colonialism. María saw the food system as an agent of colonial control and worked to reduce the reliance on foreign imports. She developed products, cooking utensils and preservation methods that are still used to this day, such as palayok clay pot ovens, and is seen as a war hero.

Her innovations not only introduced new flavours, but also economic opportunities, finding ways to export perishable foods such as frozen canned mangos and fermented pineapple juice. She also developed a nutrient-dense food called Soyalac, a soya-based powder that could be easily prepared and was used as a war food, fed to POWs in Japanese concentration camps. She has been largely forgotten, but we wanted to pay tribute to this amazing woman in *Masarap*. Salamat, María!

CALAMANSI

When eating in the Philippines, you'll find a small bowl with some tiny round green fruits no bigger than a grape, usually sitting beside a small red chilli or a tiny bowl of soy sauce. You'll see them in bowls at breakfast buffets or sitting in a repurposed plastic Hellmann's mayonnaise bucket at a street food stall on the side of a dusty road. In homes, you'll often see them picked directly off a small green bush or tree, as many families grow their own rather than buy them in bundles in a market.

You'll find this ubiquitous fruit everywhere: in drinks, in salads and served as a form of table seasoning added as a final punch of flavour to your meal. It's a citrus hybrid of a kumquat and a mandarin, with the sourness of a lemon and the look of a tiny lime with orange flesh. Its sharp sweetness is unlike any other fruit. The juice is opaque, with a bright balance of sweet–sour on the tongue. It not only wakes up your taste-buds, but I also often get a real kick of energy from the sharp taste.

Calamansi boldly finds its way into many of the classic, and best, Pinoy dishes, such as sisig, sinigang, kinilaw and pancit. It's also used as a garnish or as extra seasoning by squeezing the juice over your food, and is added to Filipino soy sauce to create toyomansi (see the next page for more on this). You also often see it in pastries and desserts, served as a juice or in cocktails. It's our favourite citrus fruit and we're making it our mission to get it the attention it deserves.

You can buy 100% calamansi juice extract in a shop called Pinoy Sari Sari off Mary Street in Dublin, which is the best option we've found in Ireland.

FILIPINO SOY SAUCE

Records show that Chinese merchant traders were present in the Philippines in the 2nd century AD. They brought fish sauce, noodles, dim sum and soy sauce. This led to the birth of Filipino-Chinese dishes such as lumpia, pancit, siopae and siu mai.

Filipino soy sauce is slightly different from standard versions. It's saltier, darker in colour and is very thin. Data Puti is a great brand that's readily available in most Asian markets.

MANG TOMAS

Mang Tomas is a pantry staple – no Filipino household is without it. It's made mainly of breadcrumbs, cane sugar, cane vinegar, garlic and pepper and is an absolute must for Pinoy pork dishes such as lechon (page 37), roast pork and lechon kawali (page 34). It reminds us of brown sauce, so if you're a fan of that, pick this one up.

TOYOMANSI

'Toyo' roughly translates to 'soy sauce' and 'mansi' is short for calamansi, so toyomansi is a mix of soy sauce and calamansi juice. This is a rich, salty, umami-packed dark soy sauce that's used in stir-fries, noodle dishes and as a seasoning and dipping sauce. My grandmother even keeps a tiny bottle of it in her bedroom, à la Nigella's iconic bedside table condiment stash. Respect.

You can buy it in Asian supermarkets. This will be a secret weapon for your cooking!

VINEGAR

Vinegar is to Filipino food as butter is to French, olive oil is to Italian or fish sauce is to Vietnamese. Vinegar is used for so much in Filipino cooking: to marinate, pickle, stew, braise and season. The Philippines is a tropical country, where temperatures rarely go below 25°C in the coldest months, which means food can go bad very quickly. Vinegars act as a flavour-enhancing preservative.

You'll find different types of vinegar across the islands: coconut sap vinegar, sugar cane vinegar and the not-as-popular palm vinegar. Many people infuse their vinegar with garlic, chillies and other dried foods, creating incredible

THE BAHAY PANTRY

Bagoong

Banana ketchup

Calamansi

Chicken powder

Crab paste

Datu Puti soy sauce

Datu Puti sugar cane vinegar

Fish sauce

Light soy sauce

Maggi All-Purpose Seasoning

Mang Tomas

Pinakurat vinegar

Shaoxing cooking wine

Toyomansi

concoctions. You'll find that many restaurants, shops and street food vendors sell their own, each a little different than the last. The best one we've had was in a restaurant near the old American army base in Clark, Pampanga, called My Lola Nor's, where we doused a deep-fried vegetable and shrimp fritter called okoy with it. It was so good we convinced them to sell us a bottle and snuck it back home in our suitcase.

In Ireland, our favourite widely available vinegar is a naturally fermented coconut sap vinegar called pinakurat that's infused with garlic, chilli and ginger. It's extremely spicy, pungent and works wonderfully in dipping sauces and dressings, to brighten up vegetable dishes and in our popular pinakurat mayo (see the recipe on page 32).

When people ask us what Filipino food is like, we often struggle to form a conclusive response. A simple, straightforward answer just will not suffice. We use words like *bold*, *punchy* and *exciting*, which are all true but not terribly helpful. Yet that's often all we can come up with to describe the cuisine that has developed and evolved from its Malayo-Polynesian roots to become a hotpot of Hispanic, American, Chinese and other Asian influences. The amalgamation of these different cultures and traditions has given rise to a wide variety of uncompromising flavours and distinctive Filipino dishes.

The culinary landscape of the Philippines has been shaped by the country's vibrant and diverse history. Spanning centuries of settlement, colonisation, trade and migration, Filipino food has evolved into a blend of indigenous flavours, alien ingredients and outside influences, resulting in the colourful cuisine we know today.

THE MALAYSIAN INFLUENCE

There is a large Malaysian influence on Filipino cuisine due to the similar ecological, geographical and cultural influences. The southern region of the Philippines – Mindanao, Samal and the Sulu Archipelago – was the entry point of the Indo-Malay ancestors and it's where you'll also see Arab and Indian influences. Spicy coconut milk dishes such as rendang, curry manok iban talum (a chicken curry with coconut milk) and ginataang manok (spicy chicken stewed in coconut milk) epitomise the Indo-Malay infusion of coconut, turmeric, ginger, garlic, lemongrass and chillies into the cooking of this region. You might see this influence in our Bahay menus in the form of palapa (a spice paste made with garlic, ginger, chilli and spring onions; see page 59) or my favourite dish, laing (kale braised in coconut milk and chilli; see page 54).

THE SPANISH INFLUENCE

A fusion of flavours commenced with the arrival of far-flung foreign powers. The Spanish colonisers, who occupied the Philippines for 333 years, introduced a plethora of ingredients and cooking techniques. Tomatoes, garlic and onions became integral parts of Filipino cuisine. Since the Spaniards arrived directly after colonising much of South America, they also brought fruits like guava, pineapple and papaya as well as avocado, corn, tomato, sweet potato and spices from the 'New World'. These were all eventually farmed in the Philippines and integrated and eaten in ways that were often vastly different from where they originated. Bay leaves and annatto seeds came from Mexico, where the Spanish ruled from, and are now so widely used in Filipino cooking that they are often assumed to be native ingredients.

A CULINARY MOSAIC

Even with all these foreign influences, Filipino cuisine retains a remarkable resilience, fiercely guarding its indigenous flavours and traditions. Regional variations reflect the country's diverse cultural tapestry, with each island, province and town contributing its distinct culinary nuances. Whether it's the fiery spices of Bicol, the fresh seafood bounty of Palawan or the delicate flavours of Ilocos, every region adds its own brushstroke to the ever-evolving portrait of Filipino cuisine.

In the creative crucible of the Filipino kitchen, where tradition and innovation collide, Filipina writer Doreen G. Fernandez observed that food becomes an expression of 'love, history, and filial duty'. It is a celebration of life, a testament to the resilience of a people and a reminder that the true essence of Filipino cuisine lies not just in the flavours that tantalise the taste-buds, but in the stories the cuisine tells and the connections it forges. With each mouthful, we partake in a gastronomic journey that spans centuries, carrying with it the echoes of indigenous wisdom and the interwoven narratives of cultures past and present.

Filipino food culture reflects the nation's history and its openness to embracing diverse influences. It is a culinary mosaic that continues to evolve as new cultures leave their mark. From the indigenous heritage to the Malaysian, Chinese, Spanish and American influences, Filipino cuisine remains a delightful fusion that honours its roots while embracing the dynamic flavours of the present.

Filipino cuisine harmoniously merges native ingredients and techniques together. It is the culinary legacy of travellers, neighbours and foreign powers that once claimed dominance over the islands. From the bustling markets of pre-colonial times and the remote fires of rural provinces to the kitchens of modern-day Filipinos, these cultural influences continue to shape and define Filipino cuisine.

At its core, Filipino food is deeply rooted in the traditions of the archipelago. The Austronesian ancestors of the Filipinos cultivated rice, fished the bountiful seas and foraged for ingredients such as coconut, bananas, taro and ube (purple yam). These staples laid the foundation for the Filipino palate, forming the base of countless dishes that are still cherished classics.

Filipino indigenous cuisine relied heavily on what was available locally and abundantly: rice, fish, seafood, tropical fruits and vegetables. The cooking reflects a close relationship with the land, utilising locally available ingredients and traditional cooking methods that have been passed down through generations. These methods are often simple and always resourceful: cooking over fire using clay pots, banana leaves and bamboo utensils.

THE CHINESE INFLUENCE

Over the centuries, Chinese merchant traders used the islands to restock, refuel and trade on their journeys. They brought soy sauce, tofu, dim sum, lumpia (page 50) and noodles with them. This Chinese impact is seen in most Filipino kitchens, particularly in street food – Chinese culinary techniques such as stir-frying and dumpling-making have become integral to Filipino cuisine. Manila has the world's oldest Chinatown, which we were lucky enough to visit on our travels. Richie's grandmother has Chinese heritage, so we see this influence first hand in her favourite foods.

WHAT IS FILIPINO FOOD?

by
Alex O'Neill

The majority of dishes prepared in Filipino kitchens today can be traced back to Spain. It's widely believed that the Spanish introduced adobo to the Philippines because the name comes from the Spanish verb 'adobar', which means 'to marinate'. However, it's now agreed that the Spanish were simply the first to name this dish after witnessing how the indigenous people cooked with vinegar. They did, however, introduce cooking methods like pan-frying, stewing and sautéing.

Most Spanish recipes have been modified with local, plentiful ingredients and adapted to Pinoy preferences. The Spanish also introduced popular baked goods and desserts like pan de sal (a yeasty, sweet roll), flan (page 60) and ensaymada as well as rice dishes and, most famously, lechon (page 37).

The Spanish also introduced Catholicism to the Philippines, which is still practised by 80% of the population today and which has had a big impact on Filipino society and cuisine. The dishes introduced by the Spanish include celebratory dishes cooked for festive feasting, fiestas and other special occasions. Food always plays a central role and huge efforts are made for every birthday, graduation and celebration, as you can see in the picture of Richie's grandmother's table at the start of the introduction.

THE AMERICAN INFLUENCE

After the revolution led by Filipino hero Rizal, in 1899 the Spanish handed the Philippines over … to the Americans. This meant that the Philippines fell under American influence and occupation at the turn of the 20th century. This brought a wave of change as more new ingredients and cooking styles made their way into Filipino kitchens. Canned goods, processed meats and breakfast cereals became popular and the concept of fast food exploded. The Filipinos, ever adaptable, assimilated these influences, merging them with their own culinary traditions. The result? A unique blend of East and West, typified by dishes like the beloved sweet spaghetti and fried chicken combo. The most obvious impact today can been seen on the streets and in the malls filled with fast food joints and sweet chains, and of course our beloved banana ketchup.

Or take the example of halo-halo. In 1902, US settlers built the Insular Ice Plant in Manila for the production of ice and frozen storage. The availability of ice allowed Japanese immigrants to make kakigōri, a shaved ice dessert. They used local sweetened beans called monggo with sugar and milk. This kakigōri variation was adopted and adapted into the now-renowned Filipino halo-halo, which means 'mix-mix'. It's a testament to the different influences in Filipino food history: Japanese sweet beans, Mexico's leche flan (introduced by Spain) and American ice topped with local fruits, colours and flavours. It's a perfect example of the blended history of Filipino food culture.

MASARAP

Tocino

BANANA KETCHUP-GLAZED WINGS

SERVES 4–6

The banana ketchup glaze on our chicken skewers (inihaw na manok) on page 18 is a winner. We loved it so much that we had to slather it on some deep-fried chicken wings. This idea came about during our pop-up in the Glimmerman, naturally. It was a no-brainer as chicken wings are such a pub staple – the perfect bite to have with a few pints.

1kg chicken wings (a mix of mids and primes if possible)

2 tbsp flaky sea salt

450ml vegetable oil, for deep-frying

FOR THE BANANA KETCHUP GLAZE:

200ml banana ketchup

50g light brown sugar

15g garlic, grated

10g ginger, grated

75ml 7up

juice of ¼ lemon

1 tbsp sugar cane vinegar

2 tbsp flaky sea salt

freshly ground black pepper

50g salted butter, cubed

TO GARNISH:

30g roasted salted peanuts, crushed

Put your chicken wings in a large bowl and sprinkle over the salt. Give the wings a good toss to coat them in the salt.

To make the glaze, put the banana ketchup, brown sugar, grated garlic and ginger, 7up, lemon juice, vinegar, flaky sea salt and two cracks of the pepper mill in a medium saucepan. Whisk together, making sure the ingredients are all well incorporated, then put the pan on a medium-low heat to warm gently. Once it's warmed through, whisk in the butter one cube at a time, making sure each cube is fully emulsified into the glaze before adding the next. Set aside.

Heat the oil in your deep-fryer (or see the note) to 160°C. Remove the wings from the bowl and pat them dry with kitchen paper to prevent any splatters when frying.

You're going to fry the wings twice here: first to cook the wings, then again to crisp them up. Working in batches so that you don't overcrowd the fryer or pot, fry the wings for 8–10 minutes, until they are completely cooked through (check them after 8 minutes). Transfer to a wire rack and cook the remaining wings.

Increase the temperature of the oil to 180°C. Have a large mixing bowl and your glaze at the ready, as this next stage happens fast.

Once the oil has reached 180°C, and working in batches again, add your wings to the hot oil. Give the fryer basket a shake or agitate the wings with tongs to prevent them

A NOTE ON DEEP-FRYING

A quick note on deep-frying at home if you're using a pot. Make sure it's a large, wide, heavy-based pot, like a casserole if you have one. Never overfill the pot – it should only be half full at most. Always be present and attentive when frying with hot oil, as things can go south if not. A thermometer is also very useful.

from sticking. Cook for 2–3 minutes, until nice and crisp. Transfer to a wire rack and cook the remaining wings.

Once all your wings are done, put them in the bowl, pour over the glaze and toss to coat.

Transfer to a serving platter or bowl and garnish with the crushed peanuts.

ADOBO

SERVES 4–6

Adobo is probably the unofficial national dish of the Philippines. It's one of those divisive dishes, kind of like how coddle is here in Dublin. It changes from household to household, but it always contains the same ingredients, more or less. Some households have their adobo with pork instead of chicken, while others prefer a dry adobo, where all the liquid has evaporated, leaving that tasty pork or chicken fat to spoon over your rice. It's a dish I have eaten all my life, and come to think of it, I've eaten a wide spectrum of adobos as my father makes many different styles. I guess it depends on what mood he's in. Here's my recipe for chicken adobo, inspired by the many versions my father has made for me.

1.5kg chicken drumsticks (or a mix of bone-in, skin-on thighs and drumsticks)

200ml soy sauce

200ml sugar cane vinegar

50g garlic, roughly chopped

6 bay leaves

15g black peppercorns

3 tbsp vegetable oil

20g dark brown sugar

275ml water

1 spring onion, thinly sliced, to garnish (optional)

TO SERVE:

steamed white rice

Put your chicken in a large mixing bowl with the soy sauce, vinegar, garlic, bay leaves and peppercorns. For the best flavour leave your chicken to marinate in the fridge overnight, but give it at least 2 hours.

Remove the chicken from the marinade and set aside on a plate. Don't discard the marinade, as it will be the basis for your sauce.

Heat a large, wide, heavy-based pot on a medium heat. Add your vegetable oil – once it starts to shimmer, you're good to go.

Working in batches, add your chicken pieces to the pot, skin side down. What you're looking to do here is develop some nice colour on the skin and render out the fat, as the chicken fat adds to the sauce and helps it to emulsify. Plus who doesn't like chicken fat? Remove the browned pieces and set them aside on a plate while continuing to brown the remaining chicken.

Add all the browned chicken back to the pot along with the reserved marinade, the dark brown sugar and the water. Stir to make sure everything is well acquainted. Crank the heat up to high and bring to the boil, then drop the heat and maintain a gentle simmer.

The chicken should take 20–30 minutes to cook, so leave it to do its thing. After 20 minutes, take a look at the chicken – it should be soft and should easily pull away from the bone. This is what you want. If it's not quite there yet, give it another 5–10 minutes. By this time, the liquid should have also reduced by more than half and become nice and thick.

To serve, grab a bowl of steamed white rice, add some chicken and drown everything in the sauce. Garnish with some thinly sliced spring onions if you like.

INIHAW NA MANOK
GRILLED CHICKEN

MAKES 15 SKEWERS

One of my earliest food memories is going with my uncle to one of the many street vendors in Manila offering a huge variety of grilled skewers with various ingredients. Pork and chicken barbecue are probably the most popular. 'Inihaw' means 'to grill' and 'manok' translates to 'chicken', and grilled chicken is pretty good. Now throw a spicy banana ketchup glaze into the equation and you've got yourself a party. Any chance we get to have a barbecue, you can be sure that there will be plenty of these on the menu. This is my version, inspired by the many skewers I've had in the Philippines and the 20-odd years I've been eating my father's.

450g banana ketchup

100g light brown sugar

35g garlic, grated

10g ginger, grated

150ml 7up

juice of ½ lemon

2 tbsp sugar cane vinegar

4 tsp soy sauce

flaky sea salt and freshly ground black pepper

1.2kg boneless, skinless chicken thighs

2 tbsp vegetable oil

Put the banana ketchup, brown sugar, garlic, ginger, 7up, lemon juice, vinegar, soy sauce, 2 tablespoons of flaky sea salt and four cracks of the pepper mill in a large bowl. Whisk together, making sure the ingredients are all well incorporated. Set aside for now.

Check the chicken for any excess sinew and small bone fragments, as there can often be some hiding, then cut the thighs into 4cm-thick pieces. Put the chicken in a large mixing bowl with another 2 tablespoons of flaky sea salt and half of the banana ketchup glaze. Give the chicken a good mix, ensuring it's all coated in the marinade. (The remaining banana ketchup will be used as a glaze when cooking, so put it in the fridge until you're ready to cook.) For best results marinate the chicken in the fridge overnight, but if you need them on the day, give them at least 3 hours.

Soak 15 wooden skewers in water for 1 hour. When you're ready to cook, take a skewer in one hand and use the other hand to thread the chicken onto the skewer one piece at a time. I usually do four or five pieces per skewer.

You can cook these in one of two ways. The best way is on a barbecue, but this is Ireland – you can't rely on the weather. But they are just as good cooked on a pan. If you've got a griddle pan, great! No sweat if not. So heat a large non-stick frying pan on a medium heat, then add

MASARAP

the oil (or brush the ridges of a griddle pan with oil). Once the oil starts to shimmer or your griddle pan is smoking hot, carefully add your chicken skewers, but don't overcrowd the pan.

Brown the skewers on both sides, then drop the heat slightly and brush the skewers with the reserved banana ketchup glaze, making sure to flip them and glaze the other side. The sugar in the glaze tends to burn quite quickly, but a bit of char is what you want. Just drop the heat to low if it's beginning to char too much. The chicken should take 8–10 minutes to cook.

Once cooked, brush the skewers with a final generous layer of the glaze, season with a pinch of salt and dig in.

CHICKEN INASAL

SERVES 4–6

This dish originates from the city of Bacolod and is hugely popular all over the Philippines. 'Inasal' roughly translates to 'char-grilled' or 'roasted meat'. Mang Inasal is a chain of fast-food restaurants that specialises in chicken inasal, with over 500 locations around the Philippines. It's kind of like a Nando's vibe but better – way better.

230ml vegetable oil

1 tbsp annatto seeds

3 lemongrass stalks, outer leaves removed

4 tbsp calamansi juice (if you must, you can use lemon juice as a replacement)

40g garlic, peeled

a thumb-sized piece of fresh ginger, peeled and chopped

1 bird's eye chilli, deseeded (optional)

75ml 7up

4 tsp light soy sauce

flaky sea salt and freshly ground black pepper

6 chicken legs

75g butter

TO SERVE:

sinangag (page 46)

Put the oil and annatto seeds in a small saucepan on a low heat. Allow the oil to infuse for 10 minutes, then turn the heat off and let it cool down. Once cooled, strain the oil into a bowl through a fine mesh sieve and discard the seeds.

Slice the lemongrass stalks into rounds and put in a food processor along with 2 tablespoons of the calamansi juice and all the other ingredients except the chicken and butter. Add 100ml of the strained oil and some salt and pepper and blend till you have a loose paste.

Take a sharp knife and make three cuts on each chicken leg: two on the thigh and one on the drumstick. This allows the marinade to penetrate and results in better seasoning. Put the chicken legs in a bowl with the paste and 2 tablespoons of salt. Rub the paste and salt thoroughly into each piece of chicken, then cover the bowl and marinate in the fridge overnight or for at least 3 hours.

Melt the butter in a saucepan, then whisk this into the remaining annatto oil. Add the remaining 2 tablespoons of calamansi juice along with 1 tablespoon of salt and two twists of the pepper mill. This will be your basting oil for the chicken. Set aside a little bit for drizzling over the chicken at the end.

Preheat the oven to 200°C (180°C fan) (or see the note if you're cooking the chicken on a barbecue).

Put the chicken on a wire rack set on top of a baking tray. Give each leg a lick of the basting oil and season

MASARAP

TRY THIS

This is best cooked on a barbecue over an indirect heat to get that proper smoky flavour. You'll need to set up your coals on one side and leave one side clear as a safe zone away from the direct heat. Use the direct heat to get some colour on the chicken, then move the chicken to slowly cook on the indirect side for 25–30 minutes, until the juices run clear or the internal temperature of the thickest part registers 75°C on a meat thermometer.

with salt and pepper. Cook in the preheated oven for roughly 25 minutes, until the internal temperature of the chicken reaches 75°C on a meat thermometer or the juices run clear. Baste the chicken with the oil every 8 minutes until it's finished cooking.

If the chicken has cooked but doesn't have any char on it, turn on your grill to full whack, give it another smooch of the basting oil and throw it under the grill until nicely charred.

Serve with sinangag, making sure you give your rice and chicken a final drizzle of the basting oil.

FILIPINO-STYLE 4 IN 1

SERVES 4–6

I love a good 4 in 1. Always have, always will. It's normally a safe option to order, as most places can't mess this up (you would hope). I always have cooked rice knocking about and usually some potatoes. I was in the mood for a 4 in 1, so I decided to make my own one day with a bagoong-laced curry sauce. There are a few steps involved and it is quite time consuming. It's a lot more convenient to just order one, but trust me, this is worth making.

FOR THE CHIPS:

2 litres water

1 tbsp fine sea salt

1kg Maris Piper potatoes, skin on

vegetable oil, for deep-frying

FOR THE FILIPINO FRIED CHICKEN:

900g boneless, skinless chicken thighs, cut into slices 1.25cm thick

2 garlic cloves, grated

1 tsp soy sauce

1 tbsp fine sea salt

freshly ground black pepper

200g plain flour

100g potato starch

First, you need to make the chips. Grab a big pot and put in the water and salt. Start cutting your potatoes into slices 1.25cm thick. Put those slices flat on the chopping board and cut them into 1.25cm batons, then put them in the pot with the water. Repeat this process until all your spuds have been chipped. Cover the pot and bring to the boil, then drop the heat to medium-low and maintain a gentle simmer for 12 minutes. Strain off the water and let the chips drain in a colander, then put them on a baking tray in a single layer to cool down for 10 minutes.

Heat the oil in your deep-fryer to 160°C (if you don't have a deep-fryer, see the note on page 15).

Working in batches, fry your chips for 6 minutes. Once all the chips have been fried, set aside on kitchen paper to absorb any excess oil.

Put the chicken slices in a bowl with the garlic, soy sauce, salt and eight twists of the pepper mill. Leave to marinate while you start working on the sauce.

Melt the butter in a medium-sized pot on a medium heat. Once the butter is melted and bubbling, reduce the heat to medium-low, add your onion and cook for about 8 minutes, until softened. Throw in the garlic and cook for 2 minutes.

MASARAP

Once everything is nice and aromatic, go in with the flour, peanut butter, curry powder, bagoong and chicken powder and cook for 3 minutes. Add half of the stock and all of the coconut milk and slowly bring up to a simmer while continuously stirring. Add the remaining stock and continue to cook for about 5 minutes, until thickened. Season with the teaspoon of salt and four twists of the pepper mill.

Blitz the sauce with a hand blender for about 3 minutes. Pass the sauce through a fine mesh sieve into another pot. This gives the sauce a silkier texture, which is what you want. Set aside.

Finally, turn the fryer up to 180°C to fry the chicken.

Combine the plain flour and potato starch in a large bowl. Toss the chicken in the flour mixture, making sure to really press it into the chicken. Shake off any excess. Working in batches, fry the chicken for about 5 minutes, until the internal temperature reaches 75°C on a meat thermometer.

Once all the chicken is cooked, have your sauce heating up in the background while you do the last fry for the chips.

Fry the chips at 180°C for 3 minutes, until golden and crisp, then put them in a large bowl and season with salt.

Take some plates or bowls and add the sinangag first. The rest of the order is up to you!

FOR THE SAUCE:

50g unsalted butter

1 large onion, diced

4 garlic cloves, minced

50g plain flour

30g crunchy peanut butter

2 tsp curry powder

1 tsp bagoong

1 tsp chicken powder

400ml chicken stock

100ml coconut milk

1 tsp fine sea salt

FOR THE RICE:

400g sinangag (page 46)

KARE-KARE
OXTAIL STEW WITH PEANUT SAUCE

SERVES 4–6

This is a proper hug in a bowl, the kind of dish that makes all your worries disappear on a cold winter night. It originated in Pampanga, the culinary epicentre of the Philippines. It is said to have come from Indian soldiers on British ships who were trying to make curry using the local ingredients available to them.

When I was a kid I wasn't a fan of this dish due to the addition of bagoong, a fermented shrimp paste – it was a bit too jazzy for young Richard. As I started to gain an appreciation for food, that all changed and this became one of my favourite dishes to cook and to eat. It takes a bit of time, but good things always do.

TO BRAISE:

3 tbsp vegetable oil

1.4kg oxtail (you might need to ask your butcher to order it in for you, as it's not hugely popular)

flaky sea salt and freshly ground black pepper

1 large onion, diced

2 large carrots, roughly chopped

120ml Shaoxing cooking wine

600ml beef stock

TO FINISH:

1 tbsp vegetable oil

1 large onion, diced

6 garlic cloves, minced

4 medium vine tomatoes, roughly chopped

If you plan to eat this for dinner, you're going to want to start cooking this at midday or you could braise the oxtails the night before.

Preheat the oven to 180°C (160°C fan). Get a large, wide, heavy-based casserole or oven-safe pot. Stick it on a medium heat and add 2 tablespoons of the oil.

Liberally season your oxtail with salt and pepper – don't be shy here! Once the oil is shimmering, gently put your oxtail in the hot oil, working in batches so that you don't crowd the pot. The aim here is to get some nice caramelisation on all sides of each piece of meat. Once browned, transfer to a plate and continue until all the oxtail has been browned.

If there is any excess or burnt oil in the pot, strain it into a heatproof bowl to cool and wipe away any burnt bits with kitchen paper. Add the remaining tablespoon of oil with the onion, carrots and a pinch of salt. Cook for about 4 minutes, until you get some nice colour on these.

Deglaze the pot with the Shaoxing wine and allow it to reduce by half, then add 600ml of the beef stock and bring to the boil. Return the oxtail to the pot along with the resting juices collected on the plate. Cover the contents

1 tbsp bagoong, plus extra to serve

2 Chinese aubergines, cubed (these can be bought in most Asian markets, but if you can't get them, use 1 regular aubergine)

300g green beans, topped and tailed

200ml beef stock

30g crunchy peanut butter

1 tbsp soy sauce

1 tbsp fine sea salt

TO SERVE:

steamed white rice

of the pot with a piece of baking paper, put the lid on and cook in the preheated oven for 3½–4 hours, until the meat pulls away from the bone with no resistance.

While the oxtail is doing its thing in the oven, you can prep the remaining vegetables.

Remove the oxtail and set aside. Strain the cooking liquid into a bowl through a fine mesh sieve, discarding the solids. Put the pot on a medium-low heat with 1 tablespoon of oil. Once it's come up to temperature, throw in the diced onion and cook for 3 minutes, until lightly browned. Go in with the garlic and cook for another 2 minutes, then add the tomatoes and cook for 3 minutes more. Add your bagoong and cook for about 4 minutes, until lightly caramelised. Add your aubergines and green beans along with the beef stock, the reserved braising liquid, the peanut butter and soy sauce and 1 tablespoon of salt. Bring to the boil, reducing until slightly thickened.

Serve on steamed rice with an extra dollop of bagoong on the side for that funk if you're into it.

TIYULA ITUM
BURNT COCONUT BEEF

SERVES 4–6

The origins of this dish are from the Tausūg people, who are considered to be one of the largest Muslim ethnic groups in the Philippines. They live in the south-western part of the Philippines, near Palawan and Sulu. This dish is a rich stew usually made with beef or goat and has a distinct dark, sometimes black colour due to the addition of burnt coconut meat.

1 x 440g tin of coconut meat, drained

5 garlic cloves, minced

40g ginger, minced

3 lemongrass stalks, outer leaves removed, minced

1 bird's eye chilli, minced (remove the seeds if you don't like too much heat)

salt and freshly ground black pepper

3 tbsp vegetable oil

1.2kg stewing beef, diced into 5cm cubes

1 large onion, diced

500ml beef stock

1 x 400ml tin of coconut milk

40ml sugar cane vinegar

40ml soy sauce

30ml fish sauce

TO SERVE:

steamed white rice

spring onions, thinly sliced

Heat your grill to its highest setting.

Put the drained coconut meat on a baking tray and put it under the grill until it turns dark brown, which should take about 5 minutes. If you want a strong coloured/flavoured end result, burn the coconut meat until it turns black. Set aside.

Put the garlic, ginger, lemongrass, chilli and burnt coconut meat in a food processor along with 1 tablespoon of salt, four cracks of the pepper mill and 1 tablespoon of the vegetable oil and blitz to a paste.

Put the diced beef in a mixing bowl and season with 2 tablespoons of salt, four cracks of the pepper mill and 2 tablespoons of the coconut paste. Give it a good mix and marinate in the fridge for at least 3 hours but overnight is best. Put the coconut paste in the fridge too.

Remove the beef from the fridge and let it come up to room temperature.

Heat 1 tablespoon of oil in a large heavy-based pot or casserole on a medium heat. Brown the beef in batches and transfer to a plate.

Add another tablespoon of oil and throw your onion into the pot along with a pinch of salt and the remaining coconut paste. Cook for 3 minutes, stirring, then add the beef back in along with the stock and the coconut milk. Bring to the boil, then cover with a lid, drop the heat and

maintain a gentle simmer for about 2 hours, until the beef is tender and the sauce has reduced to a thick consistency.

To finish, add the vinegar, soy sauce and fish sauce and give it a stir to bring everything together. Serve immediately with steamed white rice and garnish with some thinly sliced spring onions.

SATTI NA CURRY
GRILLED BEEF SKEWERS

SERVES 4–6

Satti is a dish of grilled skewered beef or chicken and a dipping sauce. It's also usually served with puto, a steamed rice cake. This dish originates from Mindanao and is somewhat related to the Indonesian satay skewers, which is why it's not usually made with pork, as this dish is of Muslim origin. This is a common breakfast dish for people in the south and you'll find numerous restaurants and stalls serving up satti all day and night. This version uses beef, but if beef isn't your thing, feel free to use chicken or pork.

FOR THE SKEWERS:

1kg striploin or sirloin steak, cut into 4cm cubes

1 garlic clove, minced

10g fresh ginger, grated

4 tsp calamansi juice

1 tsp light brown sugar

1 tbsp fine sea salt

freshly ground black pepper

2 tbsp vegetable oil

FOR THE DIPPING SAUCE:

50g unsalted butter

1 medium onion, finely diced

1 tsp fine sea salt

2 garlic cloves, minced

1 tbsp minced ginger

1 tsp bagoong

1½ tbsp curry powder

50g plain flour

1 tbsp annatto powder

400ml beef stock

150ml coconut milk

If you're using wooden or bamboo skewers, soak them in water for 30 minutes.

Put the steak, garlic, ginger, calamansi juice, brown sugar, salt and three cracks of the pepper mill in a large mixing bowl. Mix well to incorporate and set aside.

To make the dipping sauce, melt the butter in a medium-sized saucepan on a medium-low heat. Once the butter is foaming, add the onion and salt. Cook for 8–10 minutes, until the onion is softened and lightly browned, stirring every minute or so to prevent it from burning. If the pot is getting a bit too spicy and the onion is starting to burn, throw in a splash of water to bring the temperature down. Add the ginger and cook for 3 minutes. Add the garlic and cook for 3 minutes, then add the bagoong and cook for 2 minutes. Add the curry powder and cook for another 2 minutes, then finally add the flour and cook for 3 minutes, stirring.

Whisk the annatto powder into the beef stock until well incorporated. Add the coconut milk and half of the stock to the saucepan and bring to the boil while whisking. Add the remaining stock, then reduce the heat to a simmer. Cook for 3–5 minutes, until thickened. Use a hand blender to blitz the sauce until it's silky smooth. If you want it extra silky (which

you do), pass the sauce through a fine mesh sieve into a bowl after blending. Set aside until needed.

Thread four or five pieces of beef onto each skewer. Heat the vegetable oil in a medium non-stick frying pan on a medium-high heat. Working in batches so that you don't overcrowd the pan, add the beef skewers and cook for about 2 minutes on the first side, until some nice colour has developed on the beef. Flip the skewers and cook for another 2 minutes. Remove from the pan and set on a plate while you cook the rest.

To serve, warm the sauce and transfer it to a bowl to go alongside your skewers for dipping.

BISTEK
FILLY CHEESESTEAK

MAKES 4

Bistek has its origins in the Spanish word 'bistec', which translates to 'beefsteak'. Bistek consists of thinly sliced beef marinated in soy sauce, calamansi, garlic, brown sugar and black pepper that is then lightly grilled and braised in its marinade along with some sliced onions. Add a calamansi salsa verde, pinakurat mayo and a cheese sauce, and it's the perfect steak sandwich.

800g striploin or sirloin steak, cut into slices 2.5cm thick

1 tbsp light brown sugar

2 tbsp soy sauce

2 tsp calamansi juice

2 tsp sugar cane vinegar

freshly ground black pepper

2 tbsp vegetable oil

1 large onion, thinly sliced into rings and separated

1 tsp fine sea salt

4 crusty bread rolls, approx. 15cm long

FOR THE CHEESE SAUCE:

50g unsalted butter

50g plain flour

400ml full-fat milk

130g mature Cheddar cheese, grated (try to use a sharp Irish Cheddar if you can – we like Coolattin)

½ tsp fine sea salt

Put your sliced steak in a mixing bowl with the brown sugar, soy sauce, calamansi, vinegar and 15 twists of the pepper mill. Give it a good mix and set aside.

To make the cheese sauce, melt the butter in a medium-sized saucepan on a low heat. Once the butter is foaming, add the flour and cook it out for 4 minutes while stirring with a spatula. Add half of the milk, increase the heat to medium and whisk until the sauce starts to thicken. Add the remaining milk and the grated cheese, drop to a low heat and whisk until the cheese has melted and the sauce has thickened. Season with the salt and set aside till needed.

To make the salsa verde, put all the ingredients in a food processor and pulse to combine. You want to have a bit of texture, so don't over-blitz the mixture. If you don't have a food processor, mince all the fresh ingredients with a knife, then put in a bowl with the oils, calamansi, vinegar and salt and mix to combine.

For the mayo, put everything except the vegetable oil in a food processor. Turn the processor on low and slowly add the oil until it begins to emulsify. Be careful not to add too much oil at once, as you might split the mayo. Continue to slowly add the remaining oil until it's all been incorporated.

MASARAP

FOR THE SALSA VERDE:

20g fresh coriander

20g fresh parsley

1 shallot, roughly chopped

1 jalapeño chilli, roughly chopped

1 garlic clove, roughly chopped

4 tbsp vegetable oil

1 tbsp extra virgin olive oil

1 tbsp calamansi juice

1 tbsp sugar cane vinegar

1 tsp fine sea salt

FOR THE MAYO:

2 egg yolks, at room temperature

1 garlic clove, grated

2 tbsp pinakurat vinegar

1 tbsp Maggi All-Purpose Seasoning

1 tsp Dijon mustard

230ml vegetable oil

Back to the beef: grab a large frying pan and put it on a high heat. Add 1 tablespoon of the vegetable oil. When it's lightly smoking, add the onion rings and season with the salt. Cook, tossing occasionally, until the onions are nicely charred, then remove to a plate.

Wipe the pan clean with some kitchen paper and put it on a medium heat. Add the remaining tablespoon of oil. Strain the beef through a sieve but make sure you reserve the marinade. When the oil is lightly smoking, throw the beef into the pan and cook for 4 minutes, tossing occasionally. Add the leftover marinade, increase the heat to high and cook for 2 minutes, then turn off the heat but leave the beef in the pan.

At this point, reheat the cheese sauce. If you feel it's too thick, add a splash of milk to loosen it up. (Any leftover sauce will keep for about three days in the fridge.) Slice and toast the rolls. Smear a generous tablespoon of the mayo onto the top and bottom of the bread. Add some steak to the bottom half and some grilled onions to the top half. Drizzle 1–2 tablespoons of your cheese sauce over the steak, then drizzle over a tablespoon of the salsa verde. Sandwich it all together and you're ready to go. This is a messy one, so I suggest wrapping the sandwich in some foil or greaseproof paper.

FILIPINO-STYLE RIBS

SERVES 4–6

I've been eating these ribs for as long as I can remember. My dad always makes them, but interestingly, I've never had or even seen them in the Philippines. The ribs are brushed with the banana ketchup glaze used in some of the other recipes, so you know it's gonna be good gear!

2 racks of pork spare ribs or baby back ribs, silver skin removed (you can ask your butcher to do it)

FOR THE RUB:

35g light brown sugar

1 tbsp fine sea salt

2 tsp coarsely ground black pepper

1 tsp garlic powder

1 tsp smoked paprika

¼ tsp mustard powder

FOR THE GLAZE:

200ml banana ketchup

50g light brown sugar

15g garlic, grated

75ml 7up

juice of ¼ lemon

2 tbsp flaky sea salt

1 tbsp grated ginger

Whisk all the rub ingredients together. Liberally sprinkle the rub on the racks of ribs on both sides, making sure you really massage it in so that every inch of the rack is seasoned. Put the ribs in the fridge to cure for at least 3 hours or overnight if you want to cook them the next day.

Preheat the oven to 190°C (170°C fan).

Wrap each rack separately in two layers of tin foil, making sure they're tightly wrapped with no holes. Place on a wire rack set on top of a baking tray and cook in the oven for 1 hour. Remove from the oven and let the ribs rest in the foil for 15 minutes.

Turn your grill to its highest setting.

To make the glaze, put all the ingredients in a mixing bowl and whisk together to combine.

Open up the foil parcels (watch out for the escaping steam) and liberally brush the glaze over both sides of each rack of ribs. Put the racks under the grill for roughly 3 minutes to caramelise the glaze. Remove from the grill, brush both sides of each rack with more glaze and grill on the other side for 2–3 minutes. Repeat this process three more times, alternating sides, until the glaze is thick and sticky.

Cut the ribs into portions and serve immediately.

LECHON KAWALI
FRIED PORK BELLY

SERVES 4–6

You can't go wrong with some crispy pork belly – it's always a winner. A kawali is a type of wok or deep frying pan that is traditionally used to make this dish, but a deep-fryer will do the job just as well. Traditionally, it's served with a side of sawsawan, a soy- and vinegar-based dipping sauce, or good ol' Mang Tomas, which I like to think of as Filipino brown sauce – except it's usually made with a base of liver.

2 litres water

2 onions, quartered

6 garlic cloves, crushed

6 bay leaves

40g fine sea salt

1 tsp black peppercorns

1.2kg pork belly, skin on

vegetable oil, for deep-frying

FOR THE SAWSAWAN:

½ red onion, finely diced

1 bird's eye chilli, cut in half lengthways

4 tbsp soy sauce

2 tbsp sugar cane vinegar

1 tsp light brown sugar

1 tsp calamansi juice

Put the water, onions, garlic, bay leaves, salt and peppercorns in a large pot on a medium heat and submerge the pork belly in the water. Bring to the boil, then cover with a lid and drop the heat to maintain a gentle simmer. Cook for 1 hour 10 minutes. If the water level drops beneath the pork belly – which it will – just add some more water to cover the pork. Once the pork is cooked, you will be able to pierce it with a knife or skewer with no resistance.

Remove the pork belly from the water and put it on a wire rack in the fridge, uncovered. Leave it overnight to dry out the skin. This step is important as it ensures the skin is thoroughly dried before frying, which maximises the crispiness of the skin and also prevents splattering when frying.

Another important step after you've dried the pork is to take a skewer and lightly pierce the skin about 80 times all over. By lightly, I mean just until the skewer breaks the skin. This allows the hot oil to penetrate the skin and puff it up from the inside.

To make the sawsawan, combine all the ingredients in a small bowl and set aside for later.

We'll be doing a double fry to achieve that crispy skin, so preheat the oil in your fryer to 165°C.

MASARAP

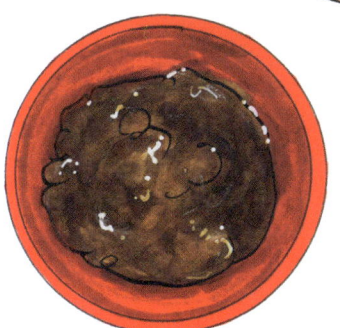

Season the skin with 1 tablespoon of salt, making sure to rub it in. Cut the belly in half or into quarters, depending on the size of your fryer. Working with one piece at a time, carefully lower the pork into the fryer and cook for 7 minutes, then drain on a wire rack. Repeat with the remaining pork.

Whack the fryer up to 190°C. Once it's up to temperature, carefully put the pork back in the fryer and cook for 2–4 minutes, until the skin has a deep brown colour.

To serve, slice the pork into strips or bite-sized nuggets and serve with a bowl of sawsawan (or just some Mang Tomas) on the side. It's also great with rice (as is everything!).

TOCINO
CURED SWEET PORK

SERVES 4–6

'Tocino' is the Spanish word for bacon, but the Filipino preparation is different. It's cured in a salt and sugar mixture, so it tends to be on the sweet side. Tocino is usually eaten in the form of tosilog – silog is a class of breakfast dishes that contain sinangag (garlic rice), fried eggs and various cuts of meat and/or fried fish. Growing up, this was my favourite breakfast to eat. I also have many fond memories of eating chicken nugget silog in the Philippines.

130g light brown sugar

4 garlic cloves, grated

juice of ½ orange

2 tbsp sugar cane vinegar

2 tbsp soy sauce

2 tbsp ketchup

1 tsp annatto powder

1 tsp smoked paprika

1 tbsp fine sea salt

8 twists of the pepper mill

1kg boneless pork shoulder, cut into slices 1.25cm thick (ask your butcher to do this for you)

1 tbsp vegetable oil

Grab a large mixing bowl and put everything in it except the pork and vegetable oil, mixing well to combine. Add the pork, stirring until it's all coated in the marinade.

Transfer the pork and the marinade into a suitable-sized container for the fridge. Ideally you want to cure the pork for three days for optimum flavour, but if you can't wait that long, you can cook it after 3 hours.

To cook, put a medium-sized frying pan on a medium heat, then add the oil. Once it's shimmering, it means it's up to temperature. Working in batches, add the pork pieces to the pan and cook for 3–4 minutes, until they've developed a nice char. Turn the pork pieces and cook for another 2 minutes, then remove from the pan.

Plate up some sinangag with a runny fried egg on top, then serve the pork alongside.

TO SERVE:

sinangag (page 46)

2 fried eggs

LECHON
PORK BELLY

SERVES 4–6

Lechon is a celebratory dish in the Philippines, usually made with suckling pig. It's common to find it on the table of most households at Christmastime. Even though the word 'lechon' is of Spanish origin, food historians believe Filipinos were roasting wild boars and pigs on spits over fire long before the Spaniards arrived. Since we can't roast whole pigs at home, this version uses pork belly.

2kg pork belly, skin on

6 garlic cloves, thinly sliced

15g ginger, grated

1 tbsp soy sauce

2 tbsp sugar cane vinegar

3 tbsp fine sea salt

freshy ground black pepper

8 spring onions, left whole

5 lemongrass stalks, bruised and left whole

1 shallot, sliced

1 fresh red chilli, sliced

Mang Tomas, to serve

Preheat the oven to 180°C (160°C fan).

Score the flesh side of the pork belly several times with a sharp knife. Season with the garlic, ginger, soy sauce, 1 tablespoon of the vinegar, 2 tablespoons of the salt and six twists of the pepper mill, making sure to rub it in. Put the spring onions, lemongrass, shallot and chilli in the middle of the belly. Roll the belly up and tie it with butcher's twine – three or four knots will suffice.

Put the pork on a wire rack set on top of a baking tray. Season the skin with the remaining tablespoon of vinegar and salt, rubbing it in. Cook the belly in the preheated oven for 3 hours, then take it out and turn up the temperature to 240°C (220°C fan). Return the pork to the oven and cook for another 10 minutes to crisp up the skin. Remove and let the belly rest for 15 minutes before slicing. Serve with a side of good auld Mang Tomas.

CRISPY PATA
CRISPY FRIED HAM HOCK

SERVES 4–6

The first time I had this in the Philippines, it blew my mind. It's a whole ham hock that's been deep-fried. Crispy and fatty, it's one of my favourite things to eat. The ham hock takes about 4 hours to cook and then needs to dry out in the fridge overnight, but it's worth the wait! This goes down nicely with some cold beers and a side of sawsawan.

1 ham hock

1 large onion, quartered

5 garlic cloves, crushed

4 bay leaves

25g fine sea salt

1 tbsp black peppercorns

1.5 litres water

vegetable oil, for deep-frying

FOR THE SAWSAWAN:

½ red onion, finely diced

1 bird's eye chilli, cut in half lengthways

4 tbsp soy sauce

2 tbsp sugar cane vinegar

1 tsp light brown sugar

1 tsp calamansi juice

TO SERVE:

sinangag (page 46)

Put the ham hock in a large pot with the onion, garlic, bay leaves, salt and peppercorns, then pour in the water. Bring to the boil, then cover with a lid and drop the heat to maintain a gentle simmer. Skim off any scum that rises to the top with a spoon, as these are impurities from within the ham hock. Simmer the hock for 4 hours but keep an eye on the water level and top it up if needed – you need just enough water so that the ham is always submerged. Once the hock is cooked, it should be easily pierced with a knife with little or no resistance.

Remove the hock and put it on a wire rack to cool down before putting it in the fridge overnight to dry out. You're also going to be double frying the ham hock to achieve maximum crispiness.

The next day, remove the ham hock from the fridge and let it come up to room temperature before frying (this should take 15 minutes).

Preheat the oil in your deep-fryer to 165°C (if you don't have a deep-fryer, see the note on page 15).

You can make the sawsawan while you wait – simply combine all the ingredients in a small bowl.

If your fryer basket is big enough to fit the hock, then use that. If not, then remove the basket and fry it directly in the well of the fryer. Gently place the hock in the fryer and

MASARAP

cook for 12 minutes, making sure to rotate the hock and move it around to cook it evenly. Remove the hock from the fryer and put it on a wire rack.

Increase the temperature on the fryer to 190°C. Once it's up to temperature, put the hock back in and fry for 2–3 minutes, until you get a deep brown colour and the skin is blistered and crispy all over. Drain the hock on a wire rack set over a baking tray and season with a pinch of fine sea salt.

I find it's best to serve this in the middle of the table with a sharp knife and a side of sawsawan and of course sinangag, then let everyone get stuck in.

KINILAW
CURED FISH

SERVES 2

Kinilaw is the Philippine's answer to ceviche, the Latin American raw fish dish. 'Kinilaw' translates to 'eaten raw'. The components of the dish can differ, from the type of fish and vinegar used to the aromatics. I absolutely love eating fish prepared this way, but you want to use the freshest fish possible. I use sea bream for my version, which I buy whole. If you're confident enough to clean and fillet a fish, work away. There's no hassle asking the fishmonger to do it for you though.

2 tsp sugar cane vinegar

2 tsp calamansi juice

200g sea bream fillets, cut into 1.25cm cubes

1 tsp fine sea salt

freshly ground black pepper

30g finely diced red onion

½ green bird's eye chilli, very finely chopped

Combine the vinegar and calamansi juice in a bowl. Put the fish in a separate bowl and season with the salt and five twists of the pepper mill, then add the red onion and chilli. Spoon over the calamansi vinegar mixture and stir everything together. Let the fish marinate and cure for about 5 minutes, then get stuck in!

MASARAP

PANCIT NA HIPON
NOODLES WITH SHRIMP SAUCE

SERVES 4

Pancit refers to a variety of noodle dishes in the Philippines. Alavar sauce was first served at the Alavar Seafood Restaurant in Zamboanga City, located in the southern part of the Philippines. Traditionally this sauce is made using the fat from native spanner crabs, which gives it a bright orange hue. Unfortunately, crab fat can't be sourced here in Ireland, but I've been known to sneak a few jars back in my suitcase from the Philippines. When I don't have crab fat, though, I use a crab paste that I buy in Asia Market in Dublin. It's nowhere near as good as the real deal, but it does the job.

500g shrimp, heads and shells on

2 tbsp vegetable oil

1 onion, quartered

4 garlic cloves, crushed

1 bird's eye chilli, halved

2 bay leaves

1 tsp black peppercorns

1.5 litres water

450g egg noodles

40g butter

1 tsp fine sea salt

freshly ground black pepper

1 tbsp crab paste

80ml coconut cream

1 tbsp calamansi juice

crispy garlic, to garnish (see page 46)

Start by peeling and deveining the shrimp. Twist and pull the head off first, then turn the shrimp upside down, split the shell between the legs and pull the shell off around the body. This should release the shell and make the rest peel off with ease. Reserve the shells! Once all the shrimp have been peeled, run your knife down the back of each one to reveal the vein, which can be removed by using your knife to pull it out. Cut each shrimp into three pieces and set aside.

Heat the oil in a large pot on a medium heat. Once the oil is lightly smoking, dump the shells in the pot and cook for 2 minutes, stirring. Add the onion, garlic, chilli, bay leaves and peppercorns and cook for 5 minutes more, then pour in the water. Bring to the boil, then drop the heat and maintain a simmer for 45 minutes, until the stock has reduced by half. This will leave you with about 600ml of stock, but you need only 150ml for this recipe. You can freeze the rest for up to a month.

Strain the stock through a fine mesh sieve into a bowl. Use a wooden spoon to crush the shrimp heads against the sides of the sieve to release as much liquid as possible – this is where most of the flavour comes from. Discard the shells and vegetables and keep the stock.

Get a pot of water boiling and cook your noodles according to the packet instructions. Drain.

While the noodles are cooking, melt the butter in a large frying pan on a medium heat. Once the butter is foaming, add the shrimp, spreading them out evenly in the pan. Season with the salt and three twists of the pepper mill. Cook for 4 minutes on one side, then flip them over and add the crab paste, stirring to combine. Add 150ml of the reserved shrimp stock along with the coconut cream and calamansi juice. Turn the heat up to full whack and boil for 3–4 minutes, until reduced to a nice sauce consistency. Add the cooked noodles to the pan, tossing to coat in the sauce.

To serve, divide the noodles among four plates with the shrimp and garnish with some crispy garlic.

SINIGANG TAHONG
SOUR SOUP WITH MUSSELS

SERVES 4–6

Sinigang is a sour soup that has many variations with meat and seafood. The traditional souring agents used are tamarind and unripe green fruits. I love sinigang and I love mussels, but I'd never seen a mussel sinigang before so I had to try it myself.

40g unsalted butter

½ leek, sliced

1 tsp fine sea salt

1 garlic clove, sliced

1kg mussels, washed and debearded (discard any that won't close when you give them a gentle tap on the counter)

100ml dry cider

1 tbsp lemon juice

FOR THE STOCK:

4 ripe tomatoes, halved

2 Granny Smith apples, quartered

1 onion, quartered

6 dried shiitake mushrooms

20g ginger, sliced

1 litre water

100ml tamarind liquid

70ml fish sauce

1 tsp black peppercorns

First, you need to make the sinigang stock. Put all the ingredients in a large pot and bring to the boil, then drop the heat to maintain a simmer for 1 hour. Strain the stock through a fine mesh sieve into a bowl, discarding the solids and keeping the stock.

Melt the butter in a medium-sized frying pan on a medium heat. Once the butter is foaming, add the leek and salt and cook for 2 minutes. Add the garlic and cook for 1 minute, then add the mussels and cider. Turn up the heat on full whack to let the cider reduce for 1 minute, then add the sinigang stock. Reduce for another 3 minutes, then give the pan a toss and add the lemon juice. When the mussels are cooked, their shells will be open. Discard any that haven't opened.

To serve, divide the mussels and the broth among your serving bowls and eat immediately.

MASARAP

SINANGAG
GARLIC RICE

SERVES 4–6

This is one of my favourite things to eat, hands down. It's so simple but so satisfying. You will always find sinangag on a Filipino dinner table, but everyone and their mother has a different way of cooking rice. A lot of people use ratios or measurements, but I never do. I just wash the rice until the water runs clear, then put it in the pan and add water until it touches the first knuckle on my index finger while my finger touches the top of the rice. This method has never let me down, whether I'm using a rice cooker or a pot on the hob. Luckily for you, though, I have recorded my measurements here for the first time.

420g jasmine rice
1 tsp fine sea salt
550ml water
2 tbsp vegetable oil
4 garlic cloves, chopped

Wash the rice in a fine mesh sieve until the water runs clear, then put it in a medium-sized pot with the salt and the 550ml of water. Put the pot on a medium heat and let the water come up to a simmer, which will take about 5 minutes. Once it's simmering, put a lid on the pot and turn the heat all the way down to its lowest setting. Cook for 10 minutes.

Meanwhile, put the oil and garlic in a separate small saucepan on a medium heat. When the oil comes up to temperature, the garlic will begin to fry and start to get some colour. You want it to be a light golden colour. This will take 4–5 minutes but keep an eye on the garlic as things can go south fairly quickly and you'll end up with bitter, burnt garlic. Strain the oil through a fine mesh sieve into a bowl and put the crispy garlic on a piece of kitchen paper to drain.

After the rice has cooked for 10 minutes, turn the heat off and let it sit for 5 minutes before taking the lid off and fluffing up the rice with a fork. Add the crispy garlic and the garlic oil you saved from earlier. Use the fork to stir it through the rice before digging in.

HOW TO
COOK AND CHILL LEFTOVER RICE SAFELY

Rice is a high-risk food as it carries *Bacillus cereus* spores, even when raw. Since there's almost always leftover rice after cooking a batch, you need to be cautious in how you cool down and store the rice. Rice left at room temperature for too long can lead to toxins being released into the rice that can cause severe food poisoning.

- Never cool rice in the pot you cooked it in.
- To cool rice properly, spread it out evenly on a flat baking tray, making sure to put it in the fridge within an hour.
- Always cool your rice before putting it in the fridge.
- When reheating rice, make sure it's piping hot and has reached a core temperature of at least 74°C.
- Never reheat leftover rice more than once.

LUGAW
SAVOURY RICE PORRIDGE

SERVES 4–6

One of the best things we ate on our most recent trip to the Philippines was a bowl of lugaw in Puerto Princesa in a little store on the side of the road. Lugaw, or arroz caldo, is a savoury rice porridge, usually made with chicken stock, garlic and ginger. An array of toppings, from fried pork or chicken to boiled eggs, go with it. It's eaten at any time of the day, including for breakfast. This is comfort food for many Filipinos and I 100% agree. It's a proper sort-the-head dish.

1 tbsp vegetable oil

150g onion, diced

20g garlic, minced

15g ginger, minced

400g jasmine rice

3.5 litres chicken stock

65ml fish sauce

1 tsp calamansi juice

1 tbsp fine sea salt

1 tsp ground white pepper

freshly ground black pepper

4–6 eggs (1 per person)

1 spring onion, green part only, thinly sliced

fried garlic, to garnish (this can be bought in Asian supermarkets)

Heat the oil in a large pot on a medium heat. Add the onion, garlic and ginger and cook for 5 minutes. Throw the rice into the pot and toast for 2 minutes, stirring, then pour in the stock and bring to the boil while still stirring. Drop the heat and simmer for 25–30 minutes while occasionally stirring to help break down the rice.

The consistency of your lugaw can be more on the soupy side or the porridge side. Personally I kind of like the porridge consistency, so I cook mine for longer, until I've reached my desired consistency. If soup is your buzz, there's no need to cook it for longer than the required time. Or cook it to whatever your desired consistency is, there is no wrong way! Season with the fish sauce, calamansi, salt, white pepper and six twists of the pepper mill. The seasoning measurements here are just guidelines – I encourage you to add as much or as little as you like.

Cook the eggs while the lugaw is simmering. Lower them into a pan of boiling water and cook for 7 minutes. Remove and run under cold water for 2 minutes to stop the cooking, then peel off the shells.

To serve, ladle into bowls. Garnish each portion with some sliced spring onion tops, some fried garlic and one boiled egg, sliced lengthways. Feel free to add more white pepper if you're into some spice. If you have any cooked meat lying around in your fridge, now is the time to add it. You won't regret it.

SINIGANG POTATO CRISPS

SERVES 4–6

I am an absolute fiend for a bag of crisps. If I open a fresh bag of 'sharing size' crisps, I'm not able to stop myself from eating the whole thing. Sinigang is a delicious Filipino soup that comes in many variations. It's unapologetically sour due to the use of tamarind and whatever unripe green fruits are available. It has a kind of salt-and-vinegar vibe, which is what made me think of using it as a seasoning for crisps. During our Glimmerman pop-up I made Jerusalem artichoke crisps with this seasoning but it works just as well with potato crisps.

I cheat a bit here on the seasoning, as making an array of dehydrated powders is quite time consuming. Pinoy Sari Sari on Capel Street in Dublin and sometimes Asia Market sell sachets of tamarind powder, which is extremely convenient and is perfect for this recipe. A mandolin or a food processor with a disc slicer attachment would also be handy for this unless you have incredibly sharp knives and serious knife skills.

2 litres water

1 tbsp fine sea salt

800g Maris Piper potatoes

vegetable oil, for deep-frying

1 sachet of Sinigang Sampalok Mix

Fill a large mixing bowl with the water and salt. Grab a chopping board and your mandolin. Adjust the blade to produce potato slices that are about 5mm thick. Slice all the spuds on the mandolin and put them in the salted water. PLEASE watch your fingers and use the finger guard! Cutting yourself on a mandolin is not a good buzz.

Preheat the oil in your deep-fryer to 165°C (if you don't have a deep-fryer, see the note on page 15).

Before frying, drain the potatoes, shaking off as much excess water as you can, then put the slices on kitchen paper to dry thoroughly. Working in batches, fry the potatoes for 4–5 minutes, until they are light golden. Tip out onto kitchen paper to absorb any excess oil. Toss the crisps in a large, dry bowl with the sinigang mix, using 1 teaspoon at a time – it's quite sour, so taste and add more if you feel it needs more.

These crisps would keep in an airtight container for about three days so you don't have to eat them all in one go, like I would.

LUMPIA
PORK SPRING ROLLS

MAKES 30

Me and spring rolls go way back – my dad has been making these for as long as I can remember. He would make them for special occasions, when neighbours came over for dinner or whenever he felt like it, really. There would usually be a stash of them in the freezer, but they wouldn't last long with me around. To this day, my friends are addicted to them because one New Year's Eve we all came back to my house after a few and there was this mountain of spring rolls that my dad had made. They're super easy to make and can be frozen for up to three weeks.

300g white cabbage, thinly shredded

200g carrots, grated

1 large onion, thinly sliced

1 tbsp fine sea salt

vegetable oil, for deep-frying

1kg pork mince

4 garlic cloves, grated

1 tbsp Maggi All-Purpose Seasoning

1 tbsp sugar cane vinegar

1 tbsp soy sauce

freshly ground black pepper

2 eggs, whisked

1 tbsp water

30 spring roll pastry wrappers (these can be bought in most Asian grocery stores)

FOR THE DIPPING SAUCE:

1 bird's eye chilli, halved

1 garlic clove, smashed

2 tbsp sugar cane vinegar

Put the cabbage, carrots and onion in a bowl and sprinkle over the salt. Give everything a good mix to incorporate the salt. Let the veg sit for about 10 minutes to let the salt draw out the moisture, otherwise you'll wind up with soggy spring rolls, which is no bueno. After the 10 minutes are up, squeeze out as much water as you can, then transfer the veg to a large mixing bowl.

Heat 2 tablespoons of vegetable oil in a large heavy-based pot on a medium heat. Add the pork, increase the heat to high and lightly brown, cooking off any excess liquid – this should take 8–10 minutes. Drop the temperature to medium-low, then add the garlic, Maggi, vinegar, soy sauce, a pinch of salt and 10 twists of the pepper mill. Cook for another 5 minutes, stirring. Put a large colander over a bowl and pour the cooked pork into the colander, allowing any fat to drain off.

Combine the drained pork with the vegetable mixture. Give it a really good mix to combine everything together.

In a small bowl, whisk the eggs together with the water to make an egg wash.

MASARAP

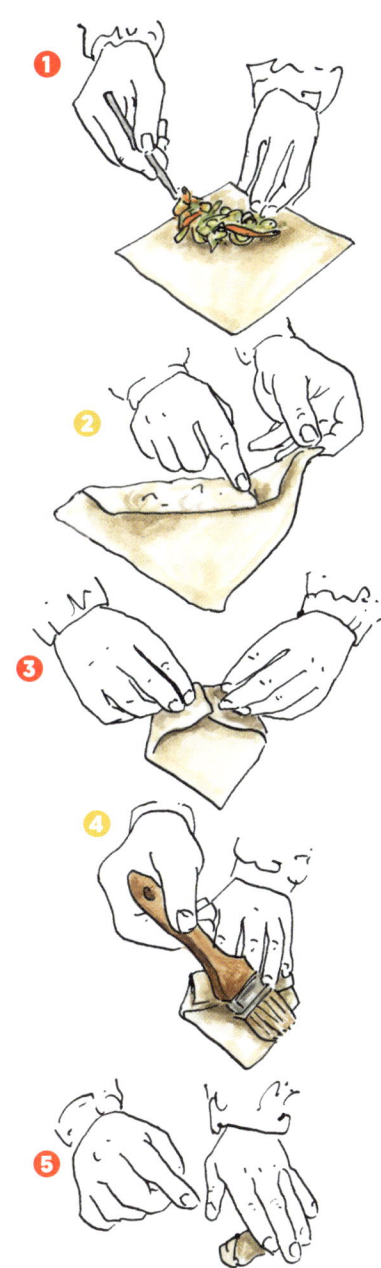

① Working with one wrapper at a time, take your spring roll pastry and turn it so that you have one corner facing you. Using a large serving spoon, portion out 50g of the filling per roll. You can weigh this out if you like, as 50g per roll will get you 30 rolls. Starting at the bottom, spoon the mixture onto the wrapper.

② Take the bottom corner and roll it away from you, making sure it's tight.

③ Keep rolling it up tightly until a cone shape has formed, then fold in the sides and tuck it in tightly by continuing to roll the wrapper forwards.

④ At this point, there should be a little lip above the conical shape you have formed, almost like an envelope. Brush this lip with the egg wash and roll the wrapper over the washed area, making sure to keep it tight.

⑤ Repeat this process until all the wrappers and filling are gone. It can be quite time consuming, especially if it's your first time making these. Recruit some friends or family members to give you a hand. I rolled thousands of these during the early days of Bahay.

Heat the oil in your deep-fryer to 170°C (if you don't have a deep-fryer, see the note on page 15).

Working with three or four spring rolls at a time, gently put them in the fryer basket. Cook for 3–4 minutes, until the rolls are light golden brown. When cooked, drain on kitchen paper and hit them with some flaky sea salt. Repeat for the remaining rolls.

To make the vinegar dipping sauce, just put all the ingredients in a bowl and give it a mix.

Serve the rolls with the dipping sauce on the side. If you have some lumpia left over, they are perfect for freezing and will keep for about three weeks. When freezing, be sure to put them in the container in a single layer and put parchment paper in between the layers.

FILIPINO FEASTS

BY ALEX O'NEILL

Filipino family gatherings are day (or night!)-long celebrations of food, eating and family that revolve around enormous tables loaded with everything you could wish for, from whole roast lechon and baked fish to mountains of prawns and mussels, roasted birds, huge bowls of rice and casseroles of lasagne and pasta. Family meals and events are basically marathon eating binges broken up with laughter, music, karaoke, gossip and catch-ups.

Vegetable side dishes are served at room temperature alongside massive portions of fish, meat and chicken. Dishes that we would consider to be desserts are interspersed with the savoury. For example, white bread dipped in hot chocolate is eaten alongside creamy pasta dishes. Diners regularly go back for more and the moment your plate looks even a little less loaded, somebody will offer you additional helpings or ladlefuls of anything you haven't managed to get to yet. Anything left over is eaten the next day for a late breakfast and lunch. It's exhausting, but at the same time you don't really want it to end.

Breaking bread for special occasions is something that Richie's family celebrates just as much in Ireland. In Richie's family, pretty much every social gathering revolves around food. You'll always find a pot of something delicious simmering away on the stove and Richie has never had a meal in his house that wasn't served family style. Every meal is a celebration shared by family and friends around the table.

There's a real intimacy and connection when you share a meal with people. It's something that is universal and transcends language, which we've experienced first-hand on our travels, but especially in the Philippines.

LAING
KALE BRAISED IN COCONUT MILK & CHILLI
SERVES 4–6

This dish originates from the Bicol region in the Philippines, which is where my grandmother is from. Traditionally it's made with taro leaves, a leafy green similar to spinach. I make mine with kale as it grows in abundance here in Ireland and is available almost all year round.

800g curly kale

1 tbsp vegetable oil

2 shallots, diced

30g ginger, grated

4 garlic cloves, grated

1 bird's eye chilli, thinly sliced (if you don't like too much heat, deseed the chilli or omit it altogether)

1¼ tsp bagoong

2 x 400ml tins of coconut milk

1 tsp fine sea salt

freshly ground black pepper

TO SERVE:

sinangag (page 46)

Strip the kale from the stalks and wash the leaves. Shake off any excess water, then tear the leaves in half. (Don't throw out those kale stalks! Our fellow Blasta author, Conor Spacey, suggests rubbing them with oil and spices and roasting them in a hot oven for about 15 minutes, until crisp, then drizzling them with natural yogurt.)

Heat the oil in a large pot on a medium heat. Go in with the shallots and ginger and cook for 2 minutes. Add the garlic and chilli and cook for another 2 minutes. Add the bagoong and cook for 2 minutes, stirring. Finally, go in with the kale, stirring to combine everything, then add the coconut milk, salt and six twists of the pepper mill. Maintain a gentle simmer for about 10 minutes, until the sauce has thickened slightly and the greens have become tender.

This dish goes well with sinangag (literally everything does!) or as a side dish with meat or fish.

POQUI POQUI
ROASTED AUBERGINES AND EGGS

SERVES 4–6

This dish hails from the Illocos Region of northern Luzon in the Philippines. I think this dish is best served as a condiment alongside grilled meats or fish, but it's also great with crackers. This recipe calls for Asian aubergines, which are longer and thinner than Western aubergines. They also contain fewer seeds, making them less bitter. You can find these aubergines at most Asian grocery stores but if you can't source them, use four regular aubergines instead.

6 Asian aubergines (or see the intro)

1 tbsp vegetable oil

¼ red onion, diced

1 ripe tomato, diced

1 garlic clove, grated

½ bird's eye chilli, finely chopped

2 eggs, whisked

1¼ tsp soy sauce

1 tsp fine sea salt

freshly ground black pepper

If you have a gas hob at home, lash the aubergines on the open flame and get them nice and charred on all sides. If you don't have gas, turn your grill up full whack and blister the aubergines under the grill. Once they're all charred, put them in a bowl or container and cover them with a lid to steam. This also makes them easier to peel. After about 10 minutes, remove the lid and peel off all the skin on the aubergines (use a paring knife if you have one). Discard the skins and keep the flesh. Run your knife through the flesh to mash it all together.

Heat the oil in a frying pan on a medium heat. Add the onion and cook for 4 minutes. Add the tomato, garlic and chilli and cook for another 2 minutes, then throw the aubergines into the pan. Add the eggs, soy sauce, salt and six twists of the pepper mill and cook, stirring, to scramble the eggs and combine everything together.

Transfer to a serving bowl and get stuck in. This dish can be eaten hot, cold or at room temperature if that's your vibe.

ATCHARA
PICKLED GREEN PAPAYA

SERVES 4–6

This pickle is traditionally made from unripe papaya along with various other vegetables like carrots and onions. Sourcing good papayas in Ireland can difficult and expensive, so you could use whatever vegetables you have lying around. It's a good way of clearing out your fridge. This is usually served alongside fried or grilled foods in the Philippines.

150g caster sugar

1 tbsp fine sea salt

300ml sugar cane vinegar

250ml water

280g carrots, julienned

150g daikon, julienned

120g onion, thinly sliced

2 red peppers, julienned

1 garlic clove, peeled and halved

1 bird's eye chilli, sliced in half

Put the sugar, salt, vinegar and water in a pot on a medium heat. Bring to the boil, stirring to make sure the sugar has completely dissolved.

If you have a 1-litre jar, put all the vegetables into it and pour over the hot liquid; otherwise, a heatproof bowl will suffice. Once the liquid has cooled down, your pickle is ready. This keeps for up to a month in your fridge in a suitable sealed container.

MASARAP

BAGOONG XO

MAKES 400G

XO sauce is a spicy seafood-based sauce that originates in Hong Kong. The seafood element is usually in the form of dried scallops and shrimps, but dried scallops are almost impossible to source here (I've been told there are legal reasons as to why they can't be imported). I absolutely love XO sauce and it's great on everything – fried rice, grilled meats, stir-fried greens … the possibilities are endless. I make my version with bagoong and guanciale. If spice isn't your thing you can deseed the chillies to mellow the heat, but what's the point in that, aye?

100ml boiling water

10g dried shiitake mushrooms

120g guanciale, cubed

4 tsp vegetable oil

2 shallots, diced

30g garlic, sliced

30g ginger, grated

80g bagoong

3 bird's eye chillies, sliced

15g dried red chillies, torn in half

20g light brown sugar

120ml chicken stock

1¼ tsp soy sauce

Pour the boiling water over the dried shiitakes in a heatproof bowl and let them soak for 20 minutes. You can prepare the rest of the ingredients while you wait.

Put the guanciale in a saucepan and turn on the heat to medium-low. As the temperature rises, the fat will begin to render out from the guanciale and it will start to crisp. This should take 8–10 minutes. Once it has become crispy, remove with a slotted spoon and drain on kitchen paper.

Keep that fat from the guanciale in the pan and add the vegetable oil. Take the mushrooms and squeeze out the water into the bowl (keep the soaking liquid). Slice the mushrooms and add them to the pan along with the shallots, garlic and ginger. Cook, still on a medium-low heat, for 6 minutes, stirring. Stir in the bagoong and cook for 3 minutes. Add the bird's eye and dried chillies and cook for 3 minutes more. Add the brown sugar, chicken stock, soy sauce and the soaking liquid from the dried mushrooms. Turn the heat up full whack and bring to the boil. Keep boiling on a high heat for 5 minutes to reduce, then turn off the heat and stir everything together.

Transfer the mixture to a food processor and blitz till you have a paste-like consistency. This paste will keep in the fridge for about a week.

PALAPA
TOASTED COCONUT SPICE PASTE

MAKES 150G

I came across palapa while researching Filipino food in the early days of Bahay. It's a sweet, spicy condiment that originates from the Maranao people of Lanao del Sur in the southern part of the Philippines. The use of sakurab, a native spring onion, and charred coconut meat is what really gives the paste its flavour. Since we don't have access to sakurab or fresh coconuts I use spring onions and tinned coconut, but you could use dried coconut flakes if you can't get the tinned kind. My version is by no means traditional but a friend of mine from Mindanao has given it his stamp of approval (nice one, Ted!).

Palapa is most commonly used in piaparan, a chicken dish that uses the paste as a base for the sauce.
It's also often eaten with condensed milk and used as a salad dressing. This paste can be used as a marinade for meat and fish, stir-fried with some greens or used as a condiment.

25g tinned coconut meat

4 tbsp vegetable oil

1 bunch of spring onions, white parts only, thinly sliced

20g garlic, finely chopped

10g ginger, finely chopped

6 bird's eye chillies, thinly sliced

40g caster sugar

2 fresh lime leaves, sliced (can be bought in Asian grocery stores)

Preheat the oven to 185°C (165°C fan).

Put the coconut meat on a small baking tray and toast in the preheated oven for 8–10 minutes, until it's golden brown.

Heat the oil in a medium pot on a medium heat. Add the spring onions, garlic and ginger and cook for 4–5 minutes, until fragrant. Stir in the chillies and cook for 1 minute. Finally, add the sugar, toasted coconut and lime leaves. Cook for 2–3 minutes, until the sugar has dissolved.

This can be stored in a jar in the fridge for up to a month.

LECHE FLAN

SERVES 4–6

Leche flan is a Filipino dessert that was brought by the Spaniards, who colonised the Philippines for over 300 years. 'Leche flan' translates as 'milk custard'. It's essentially a steamed milk pudding with a clear caramel topping. Leche flan differs from a Spanish crème caramel as it's made with condensed milk and egg yolks, which results in a super-rich custard. In some parts of the Philippines, it would have traditionally been made with the milk of the carabao, a native water buffalo. This recipe comes from my grandmother, Myrna. I ate a lot of it during my holidays in the Philippines.

280g caster sugar

2 tbsp water

10 egg yolks

1 x 410ml tin of evaporated milk

1 x 397ml tin of condensed milk

250ml double cream

1 tsp pure vanilla extract

300ml boiling water

First, you need to make the caramel and let it set. Have four lyanera pans or one 23cm baking dish close by (see the note), as you'll need to move quickly here.

Put the sugar and 2 tablespoons of water in a small pot on a medium heat. Once you see the water begin to bubble, the sugar will slowly start to caramelise. You need to fluctuate the heat between low and medium to ensure you don't burn the caramel. Swirl the pot around to ensure even caramelisation – do not stir! Swirling is the best method IMO.

You will start to see the sugar turn a nice amber colour as it turns into caramel – this could take 6–8 minutes. If you have an instant-read thermometer or a candy thermometer, take a reading – it should be around 148°C. Working quickly, pour the caramel into your lyanera pans or baking dish, swirling to spread the caramel out evenly. Leave to set.

To make the custard, put the egg yolks, evaporated milk, condensed milk, double cream and vanilla in a large bowl. Using a whisk, break the egg yolks and give it all a light mix. You don't want to incorporate too much air into the mix, as you'll be left with air bubbles, which you don't want. Switch to a spatula and gently fold the mixture until everything is well incorporated.

Using a fine mesh sieve lined with cheesecloth, pass the custard through it into a clean bowl. This ensures that the custard has a silky-smooth texture.

LYANERA

In the Philippines, leche flan is baked in an oval-shaped pan called a lyanera or llanera, which you can buy in the Pinoy store on Capel Street in Dublin for cheap. I recommend doing this if you plan on making this recipe, as it requires four of these pans. However, you could use a 23cm round baking dish and make one large flan.

Preheat the oven to 180°C (160°C fan).

Divide the custard evenly among your lyanera pans and cover each one tightly with tin foil. Put a wire rack in a deep roasting tray and put the pans on the rack. Pour the boiling water into the tray, cover the tray loosely with foil and bake in the preheated oven for 28 minutes.

Remove the tray from the oven and let it sit for 10 minutes, then remove the foil from the top of the tray as well as the lyanera pans. Cool at room temperature for at least half an hour before refrigerating the puddings for at least 4 hours, until the custard has set. You will know it's ready when there is still a slight wobble and the custard is firm to touch.

To serve, unmould the puddings by running a knife around the edges and inverting onto a plate.

FILLY LIBRE

MAKES 1

When I first started going out to clubs, they always had these two-drinks-for-€10 deals. I would always opt for the Cuba Libre, a rum-based drink with lime and Coke. Super simple but so good. During our Hen's Teeth pop-up in Dublin, our take on the Cuba Libre was in a slushy form, the Filly Libre. Same buzz but we added calamansi into the equation and my god, it's good.

65g caster sugar

20ml water

70ml calamansi juice

50ml Havana Club dark rum

4–5 ice cubes

2 lime wedges

230ml Coke

First you need to make the calamansi simple syrup. Put the sugar and water in a pot on a medium heat and stir to dissolve the sugar. Once dissolved, take the pan off the heat, add the calamansi juice and let it cool down.

Measure the rum and 25ml of the simple syrup into a glass. Add the ice, squeeze the lime wedges into the glass and drop them in too, then top up the glass with the Coke. It's that simple! You'll have some calamansi simple syrup left over, so pour it into a jar and it will keep for a few weeks in the fridge.

WHITE FILIPINO

MAKES 1

This is a tongue-in-cheek take on the classic white Russian. My love affair with white Russians goes back to when I was on holiday in Budapest seven or eight years ago. I had a serious case of heartburn and wasn't able to drink any other cocktails, as they usually contain limes or something acidic. The white Russian was my saviour on that holiday and I've loved them ever since. I've changed my version up slightly, using coconut cream instead of cream or regular milk. This is a stiff drink, which is just how I like it, but feel free to use less vodka.

50ml good-quality vodka

50ml coconut cream

25ml Kahlúa

4 ice cubes

Measure all the ingredients into a cocktail shaker and shake for 30 seconds. If you don't have a cocktail shaker, put everything in a tall glass and give it a good stir. Pour into a tumbler and enjoy.

MASARAP

BLASTA BOOKS #8

A LOVE LETTER
TO FILIPINO FOOD & THE PEOPLE WHO COOK IT
BY ALEX O'NEILL

When I first learned that Richie was half Filipino, it didn't seem like something he was attached to or even thought much about. I thought it was cool, but on hearing that he didn't speak Tagalog, hadn't been back to the Philippines in a while and didn't really have any plans to go either, I sensed how distant he was from this side of himself. I thought it was an interesting part of his family background but it didn't have a major impact on who he was. At the time, I think this is how he felt about it too.

One thing that was obvious, though, was his love of food. It was actually food that got us talking when we met backstage while Kerri Chandler was DJing at a festival that friends of ours used to run in Glendalough. More specifically, we talked about how to make a good soup. Shouting over the kick drum, we agreed that being able to make a good soup is a sign of a decent cook. But what were the steps involved in getting there? Mirepoix cooked in Irish butter, loads of salt and pepper. I said you could use stock cubes, but Richie of course disagreed. I preferred smooth, he was partial to chunky. I'm sure we talked about other things, but that conversation is what still sticks out in my memory.

Every date we went on revolved around food. On our first date we got some Japanese food in a basement in the city centre. On our second date we headed to Skinflint, where we first discovered chilli honey drizzled over fior di latte. By date three, I decided to impress him by inviting him to a spot on George's Street that I still cringe at to this day. My intention was to show off my deep gastronomic understanding, but we ended up in a room with air that scratched our throats and made my eyes sting. We laugh at it now, but he still gives me stick about it sometimes.

Food has always played an important part in our relationship, from our earliest trips abroad together to our times travelling across Ireland. Every place we go revolves around what we are going to eat there, trying new things and searching out local specialities and classic dishes.

Food can evoke such a strong sense of nostalgia and can unlock memories so powerfully that you can feel transported in mind, body and soul back to a place you thought you'd forgotten. A dense, crisp Sicilian slice with burnt, brittle bits of cheese transports me back to a dusky November evening in Brooklyn. A mouthful of a heaving Turkish kebab, where the sauces drip down my arm and the shredded salad falls on the ground in front of me, takes me to a summer break in Berlin. A spoonful of creamy coconut gising gising drops me right back to a dinner in Manila with Richie's cousins.

Today, Richie's Filipino heritage is a core part of his personal and cultural identity; it's a huge part of who he is. It's allowed him to connect deeply with other Irish-Filipinos and has given him the chance to get even closer to his father. His home life and work life have blended into each other in the kitchens he shares with his dad, Lito, at all the events he has helped us out with. Food has been the cultural lens through which he has explored his Irish and Filipino identity, an identity he continues to figure out and expand upon. Food was the catalyst for him to rediscover this part of himself.

This book is our little love letter to Filipino food and the people who cook it. We dedicate this book to the millions of overseas Filipino workers whose lives are dedicated to sending money home to support their families; to the street vendors who sell their specialities on the side of the busiest expressways I have ever seen; to the fishermen who cook freshly caught fish on wooden barbecues on their hand-built boats in the islands of Palawan; to the grandmothers who lay out the food-laden tables for all their Noche Buena children and grandchildren; to the kusineros in the slums who cook rice for their communities; to the young Filipino chefs who are making a name for Filipino food globally; and to the immigrant parents who are teaching their second-generation children about their rich Filipino heritage through the celebration of Pinoy cooking at home. This book is for you.

INDEX

A
annatto 8
aubergine
    poqui poqui (roasted aubergines and eggs) 55

B
bagoong 8
    bagoong XO 58
banana ketchup 8–9
    banana ketchup-glazed wings 14–15
    Filipino-style ribs 33
    inihaw na manok (grilled chicken) 18–19
beef
    bistek (Filly cheesesteak) 30–2
    kare-kare (oxtail stew with peanut sauce) 24–5
    satti na curry (grilled beef skewers) 28–9
    tiyula itum (burnt coconut beef) 26–7

C
calamansi 4, 5, 9–10, 11
carrots
    atchara (pickled green papaya) 56
cheese
    bistek (Filly cheesesteak) 30–2
chicken
    adobo 16–17
    banana ketchup-glazed wings 14–15
    chicken inasal 20–1
    Filipino-style 4 in 1 22–3
    inihaw na manok (grilled chicken) 18–19
chilli
    laing (kale braised in coconut milk and chilli) 54

coconut
    laing (kale braised in coconut milk and chilli) 54
    palapa (toasted coconut spice paste) 59
    tiyula itum (burnt coconut beef) 26–7
crab
    aligue 8

D
daikon
    atchara (pickled green papaya) 56
drinks
    Filly libre 62
    white Filipino 62

E
eggs
    poqui poqui (roasted aubergines and eggs) 55
    tocino (cured sweet pork) 36

F
fish
    kinilaw (cured fish) 40
flan
    leche flan 60–1

G
garlic
    sinangag (garlic rice) 46

K
kale
    laing (kale braised in coconut milk and chilli) 54

MASARAP

M
Mang Tomas 10
milk
    leche flan 60–1
mussels
    sinigang tahong (sour soup with mussels) 44

N
noodles
    pancit na hipon (noodles with shrimp sauce) 42–3

P
papaya
    atchara (pickled green papaya) 56
peanuts
    kare-kare (oxtail stew with peanut sauce) 24–5
pork
    crispy pata (crispy fried ham hock) 38–9
    Filipino-style ribs 33
    lechon (pork belly) 37
    lechon kawali (fried pork belly) 34–5
    lumpia (pork spring rolls) 50–2
    tocino (cured sweet pork) 36
potatoes
    Filipino-style 4 in 1 22–3
    sinigang potato crisps 49

R
rice
    Filipino-style 4 in 1 22–3
    how to cook and chill leftover rice safely 47
    lugaw (savoury rice porridge) 48
    sinangag (garlic rice) 46

S
salsa verde
    bistek (Filly cheesesteak) 30–2
sandwich
    bistek (Filly cheesesteak) 30–2
sawsawan
    crispy pata (crispy fried ham hock) 38–9
    lechon kawali (fried pork belly) 34–5
sea bream
    kinilaw (cured fish) 40
shrimp
    pancit na hipon (noodles with shrimp sauce) 42–3
skewers
    inihaw na manok (grilled chicken) 18–19
    satti na curry (grilled beef skewers) 28–9
soup
    sinigang tahong (sour soup with mussels) 44
soy sauce 10
stew
    kare-kare (oxtail stew with peanut sauce) 24–5

T
toyomansi 11

V
vinegar 11–12

Nine Bean Rows
23 Mountjoy Square
Dublin, D01 E0F8
Ireland
@9beanrowsbooks
ninebeanrowsbooks.com

Blasta Books is an imprint of Nine Bean Rows Books Ltd.
@blastabooks blastabooks.com

First published 2023

Copyright © Richie Castillo and Alex O'Neill, 2023

ISBN: 978-1-9993799-8-8

Editor: Kristin Jensen

Series artist: Nicky Hooper
nickyhooper.com

Designer: Jane Matthews
janematthewsdesign.com

Artwork in 'What is Filipino food?': Alex O'Neill

Proofreader: Jocelyn Doyle

Printed by L&C Printing Group, Poland

The paper in this book is produced using pulp from managed forests.

All rights reserved.

No part of this publication may be copied, reproduced or transmitted in any form or by any means without written permission of the publishers.

A CIP catalogue record for this book is available from the British Library.

10 9 8 7 6 5 4 3 2 1

About the authors

Richard Castillo was born and raised in Dublin to an Irish mother and a Filipino father. For 10 years he worked in various kitchens at home and abroad, but after the pandemic threw the restaurant industry into chaos, he wanted to play by his own rules, go back to his roots and harness his creativity to create something personal and true to him.

Encouraged by Alex, Bahay was born. Named after the Tagalog word for house/home, Richie focuses on introducing people to Filipino flavours using Irish ingredients as well as highlighting Irish-Filipino culture through food, music and art in unique spaces, locations and venues across the country.

Not content with just one project, shortly after Bahay was created, Richie began studying for a master's in psychotherapy, which he will complete in 2024. For Richie, this book was a catalyst for exploring and connecting with his Filipino and Irish heritage as well as a time of great personal growth and development.

Alex O'Neill is a food lover with a passion for exploring the past, present and future through art, language, culture and cuisine. She comes from a family of social revolutionaries, artists and engineers. She has worked in IT for the last eight years, but it was only after commencing a master's in digital marketing in 2020 that she saw the potential in the online space to foster a creative, new and alternative approach to market the idea of Bahay and introduce a wider audience to the incredible Filipino flavours that Richie explores.

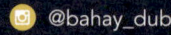 @bahay_dub